Catharsis

Shannon O'Rourke

BookLeaf
Publishing

India | USA | UK

Presentation by *BookLeaf Publishing*

Web: www.bookleafpub.com

E-mail: info@bookleafpub.com

ISBN: 9789363306080

First edition 2024

First and foremost, I want to thank my brother-in-law, Owen Riley, for his incredible creativity in designing the beautiful cover for this book. Please check out more of his masterpieces on Instagram: @owen.riley.art

A heartfelt thank you to my brother's godmother, Lorraine Latchford, for inspiring the title of this book. When I shared Survivor's Testament with her, she simply said it was "cathartic." I am forever grateful for your input and unwavering support.

To my nieces, nephews, and my two children: you are the reason I am still here and able to publish this book. You have taught me the true meaning of unconditional love. You are, and always will be, my strength and my reason to keep going. I hope I've taught you to never settle for less than you deserve, to stand up and speak out, no matter how hard it may seem. Never let anyone steal your peace, and always remember how much I love you all.

To my brother and sister, Ryan and Taylor-Jayne: thank you for being the light that guided me through the dark. You've been incredible role models, showing me what healthy relationships look like. I am so proud of the brilliant people and amazing parents you've become, despite the odds that were stacked against us.

To my father, who has always supported and believed in my poetry, even when sharing it made me feel vulnerable. Thank you for your endless love and support for me and my children.

To my mother, I am grateful for the good qualities I inherited from you and for the lessons you've taught me.

To my Nan Shirley and my Auntie Tina, who are sadly no longer with us: thank you for always answering our calls for help as children. Even after you left this earth, you answered my prayer during my darkest hours. I wrote about this in one of my poems, Prayer for Survival. Shortly after I prayed during the attack, he began to feel sick and fell asleep in my bed, giving me the chance to flee with my children. I am eternally grateful to you both. You are forever loved and missed, my angels.

To my readers: if you are facing abuse in any form, please step away and report it. You deserve more, you deserve justice. There is life after abuse. You never know what another person is capable of, and you never know if you'll be lucky enough to walk away next time.

ACKNOWLEDGEMENT

Though my childhood was unpleasant and traumatic, I am also grateful to my parents for shaping the woman and mother I have become.

My parents are wonderful people in their own ways, though they were incredibly toxic together. My mother is kind and thoughtful when she is not under the influence of alcohol. My father is a loving dad and granddad who supports me and my children unconditionally. They were both doing the best they could with what they knew at the time, and they've grown as individuals since then. I now maintain healthy relationships with both of them separately.

Despite everything, my brother, sister, and I are living proof that it is possible to break the cycle. We could have turned out so differently, but we chose a different path.

The poems in this book are based on my personal experiences with domestic abuse during childhood, sexual assault in my late teens, the murder of my aunt, and the subsequent loss of my grandmother, who passed away from grief. In my late twenties, I also faced domestic

violence at the hands of my daughter's father.
The poems explore that assault and its aftermath.

PREFACE

I am 30 years old, the youngest of three siblings, and now the mother of two young children. Growing up, my brother, sister, and I found ourselves in the middle of what felt like a never-ending warzone. The bond between my siblings and me is one I will forever treasure. We went through it all together, and no one else will ever truly understand what it was like for us. We were forced to grow up far sooner than we should have, with my siblings often stepping into parental roles for me. To this day, they remain a vital part of my support system.

As children, we were never able to fully relax and just be kids. Alcoholism was a major issue in our family, and domestic abuse seemed to be a recurring pattern passed down from generation to generation. But that cycle ended with us.

Unlike most children who hope their parents stay together, we begged for ours to separate and end their toxic relationship. That wish wasn't granted until my 21st birthday. People often say to stay together for the children, but I strongly disagree with that sentiment. It can be far more harmful for children to grow up in a home fueled by adrenaline, anxiety, and a poor example of what a relationship should be.

Throughout my life, I've made mistakes—whether in romantic relationships or by choosing toxic friendships. I was searching for love in all the wrong places because I lacked self-love and self-worth. I ignored red flags because I always tried to see the best in people. What I once thought was a great quality nearly cost me my life.

Now, I am in the process of rebuilding after a horrific assault by my ex-partner, the father of my daughter. It was the first and last time he ever laid hands on me because I refused to let my children experience even a fraction of what I went through as a child.

I am incredibly grateful to have survived the assault and to still be here for my children, who mean the world to me. I am also thankful that they were too young and asleep in bed to witness any of the attack. Despite the challenge of fleeing my home with three fractured ribs and two small children, I managed to get us to safety. I reported the offender as soon as we were safe.

Prisoner of Pain

1

Physically scarred,
Mentally barred,

Like a prisoner,
With no visitor.

Echoes of Past Wounds

Why burden me with your past sins?
When I am already damaged from your past
actions.
Lonely children crying within,
Just to know it was in vain, for your own
satisfaction.

I fear letting you in,
as every time you turn me inside-out.
Struggling with relationships and letting love in,
Being my self is all I doubt.

Jars of Emotion

3

No wonder I am scarred,
From this up-bringing.

Leaving my feelings jarred,
Made me so unhinging.

Puppets in a Storm

Insides dread, the same insides I thought was
long dead.
A puppet to your will, your judgment echoing in
my head.

Did you believe that because we were warm,
clothed, and fed,
It was acceptable for us to lie, fear-stricken, in
our bed?

Speaking of fed, we saw them often,
A few times a week—how could you not spot
them?

Children clearly deprived of safety, kindness,
and care,
Parents lost in addiction, their love laid bare.

Destroying families across the land,
Does the government even understand?

Shop shelves is where this poison is sold,
Let's go have "fun" as we are told.

How could you sleep so soundly, I'd wonder,
Leaving three young children in the middle of
thunder?

The Souls Price

You are not in control,
I understand that.

It consumes your soul,
And that's a fact!

Unfulfilled Motherhood

A mother is meant to nurture,
To hold you close, not wound you deeply.
A mother is meant to fight for you,
Not against you, not turn you into a casualty of
cruelty.

A mother is meant to foster peace of mind,
Not leave you doubting your every line.
She's meant to build you up with love,
Not tear you down, as though you're never
enough.

A mother is meant to discipline with care,
Not make you a survivor of torment's cruel
snare.
"You're fat, I wish I'd aborted you, it's your
fault he left"—
But was it really me, or the bottle you couldn't
forget?

A mother is meant to comfort and soothe,
Not make your heart race as the floorboards
move.
I hear her stir, and sickness churns inside—
Wishing for somewhere, anywhere, to hide.

Who will be the target tonight?
Which of us do you wish to fight?
Whether physical, emotional, or in the mind—
The pain lingers, though only some scars remain
behind.

A mother is meant to care, to be aware—
Yet I vanished for weeks, and you weren't there.
No call, no text, no sign of concern,
Just you at home, with another bottle to burn.

A mother is meant to teach and guide,
Not raise a hand, or crush your pride.
To have my mother beside me when I became
one too—
That support is a dream I never knew.

It's easier to forget you exist,
Than battle the voice of negativity that persists.
All the things a mother is meant to be—
But you chose not to fulfil that destiny.

Silence and Survival

I've endured abuse in countless ways,
Sexually, mentally, physically—on far too many
days.

I felt cornered, without a choice, I felt trapped,
without a voice,
As you stole a piece of my soul, a fragment I can
never rejoice.

The fear of death loomed larger than rape,
So I stayed silent as you take.

How could you find pleasure in this
unreciprocated activity?
But it was control you craved, exploiting my
naivety.

Searching for love, always lost, never found,
Believing all I deserved was to be six feet
underground.

I felt less than human, haunted by the pain,
Reliving the nightmare again and again.

These men I have to forgive,
For my own health or I shall not live.

Inherited Trauma and Loss

I never knew stability or unconditional love,
No sacrifice for us children, just a selfish mom.
Grew up in a combat zone,
PTSD, fear of every tone.

At seven years old, I couldn't bathe in peace,
I'd submerge my ears in water for a moment's
ease.
But all it did was give emphasis,
To you scream "Are you taking the piss?"

Anxiety and adrenaline-filled,
Children in fear, wondering if one parent would
be killed.
In a battle of self-destruction,
Our self-esteem needed reconstruction.

Mom turned to drink, her favored drug,
Auntie Tina gave us hope and endless love.
Until 2015, when her husband took her away,
We wondered, "Are we condemned to live in
hell, come what may?"

My Nan treated me like a daughter,
And as a mother I thought of her,

Until her own daughter, my Auntie T, was
murdered—
Her health declined, refusing to live without her.

Cancer ravaged her body, grief her silent foe.
A broken heart can kill, this I know.
As far as I see, that man committed two sins—
He took both a life and the will to live within.

In Memory of a Life Taken

Nine years ago, you were taken from our grasp,
I wished you had nine lives, to escape death's
clasp.
Beaten, pierced with knives—how it pains me to
know,
How you fought so fiercely, refusing to let go.

Two children left behind, an army of friends and
kin,
You were far too young for your life to dim.
Your body bore the marks of your brave defence,
While we uncover the killer's pretence.

Blame cast on your son, cruel and cold,
The same son who couldn't believe the story
told—
Of a stepdad's betrayal, his deadly act,
To the woman we knew as the best mom, intact.

He went to work, attempting to erase the crime,
While you lay bleeding, losing your precious
time.
We've never been the same since,
This time of year, we always reminisce.

What could have been, what should have been,
How we ache to see you again, pristine.
To hear your voice would be a dream fulfilled,
To stitch the seams of our hearts, once stilled.

There's a gaping hole in both past and future,
Where you would have been the family's suture.
Losing you riddled Nan with tumours,
What is God's will? He has no sense of humour.

In Loving Memory of Shirley Glasgow &
Tina Montgomery.

The Devouring Disease

Addiction is a cruel disease
It takes who you love
And dissolves them with ease.

Survivors Testament

Broken and bruised,
Used and abused.
Hurt me as you do,
For the drugs you misuse.

Less light behind my eyes,
With you I've severed ties,
I Pleaded and I cried,
All you did was feed me lies.

If you loved me too,
You wouldn't do what you do.
Giving birth, where were you?
Cheating, my intuition, true.

 At 3am ,on our 11 day old daughter,
You thought that you aught to,
Bring a knife and attempt to slaughter,
The mother of your youngest daughter.

For 9 months I carried her to safety,
You missed our newly born baby,
You made me your casualty,
Screaming smashing things acting crazy.

Blood leaked from my head on to the floor,
licked it from your fingers with no remorse.
How you love a blood sacrifice, I was sure,
By the devil, you were endorsed!

Told you I need medical attention,
you respond "to help me was not your intention"
You wished I died giving birth did I mention?
How could you do this to me? No
comprehension.

Nose popped, and a swollen jaw,
Glass and blood they covered the floor,
Locked in and blocked the door,
Why in my home, you declared war?

Head butted, punched and slapped,
Yet still I did not react,
For countless times I was attacked,
But these charges? I will not retract!

Trying to put a lit cigarette in my eye,
Blinded me with brandy and your lies,
Praying not to hear our baby cry,
To trust you was almost my demise.

Hands round my throat and tighter they grow,
Breathless believing this is my time to go,
Your knee to my head, blow after blow.

I am alive, now you must reap what you sow.

Knife to my chest,
And filled with threats,
While your dripping out with sweat,
spitting at me, pure disrespect!

The same knife slapped up my face,
And you left a trace,
My Nans vase you deface,
Ur next actions I anticipate.

Glasses flying and I'm the target,
"Please will you just stop it,
Which one of us is going to profit,
From this war zone, let's be honest?"

Three Broken ribs and out I bled,
Cuts to my feet and to my head,
Attacked me then you went to bed,
Your heart and conscience must be dead.

I kept calm and formed a plan,
How to escape at 6am,
With 2 children under 3 an
Pray they're as quiet as they can.

Tip toeing to get our baby from her cot
A memory that will never be forgot,

and how it thickens the plot.
Beating your child's mother, a cheap shot.

In love with a person that you inflicted,
Now I grieve someone who never existed,
You're mind must be so twisted,
I had to live for my children, so I resisted

A family we could of been,
Yes he planted that seed.
Now as my bruises they turn green,
I encompass a reflection I've never seen.

Yes the bruises they fade,
Where your hands were once laid,
My life you wanted to trade,
When you came armed with that blade.

Yet you're playing victim to the system,
Men I sure know how to pick 'em!
Now my words they are my wisdom
Night mares, how will I rid them?

I hope you're enjoying that cell,
Cause you put me through hell,
Thought that I would never tell,
That morning, you broke the spell.

To my daughter,

I pray that you're not his karma,
As I teach you no man should ever harm ya.
Because the man who tried to kill me…
He is your father.

Orphans at Dawn

The morning that nearly turned in to mourning!
The morning when my children nearly woke as
orphans.

What if he killed me, left me cold and dead?
How long would my children be crying in their
beds?

Would he have any care for them, would he
show any remorse?
Or would they follow me next, in a hearse on
that same course?

Prayer for Survival

21

Please help me I can't die and leave my babies behind.

Please do something, anything to help get me out of here alive!

Beneath the Blue Lights

I endured such a vicious beating,
Once out of sight, my home retreating.
With my two-year-old held tight in arm,
And my newborn safe from further harm.
The paramedics' words cut deep and cold:
"These battle signs show wounds untold."

I thought I'd survived, my battle done,
But fractures may mean death's begun.
I left my children with family near,
As blue lights flashed, and hope turned to fear.
And tragically, I realised late,
I might not escape death's cold debate.

Lost and confused,
yet still so infused,
I asked the paramedic, "Will my children be
taken from me?"
She replied, "No, anyone can see,
You did the best thing for them, setting them
free.

Shortly after, we arrived at the trauma centre,
Lying flat, ceiling lights greet me as I enter.

The paramedic stood close, wiping tears from
my eyes,
Gently explaining what's next, with no lies.
They work to clear my C-spine first,
Before allowing me to sit, or quench my thirst.

Several doctors, voices overlapping endlessly,
I lay still as they analyzed my wounds tirelessly.
Blinded by the lights, I strain to regain my sight,
Attempting to give my statement to the officer
stood to my right .
X-rays and MRI scans to confirm the diagnosis,
How grateful to learn my skull is not fractured,
yet the suffering feels atrocious.

Hearing that my home is now a crime scene, I
feel the weight of what this means,
A life disrupted, torn apart, unraveling at the
seams.
I realise that once discharged, it's the last place
I'll go,
Back to my dad's house, where we'll be safe, I
know.
Broken ribs have me cursing with every
movement,
when will I feel some improvement.

My sister had my daughter the first night after
the attack;

At 11 days old, I felt guilty, wanting her back.
I woke the next day, struggling to rise,
Crying my heart out as my two-year-old son
grabbed my hand and tried.
When my daughter was returned to me that day,
I panicked, wondering how I'd care for her this
way.

My father took time away from work,
To help us through and ease the hurt.
Each night, I'd wake to rustling at my bed's end,
Seeing him cradle her, my grateful heart would
mend.
My ears were dulled, so her cries I didn't hear,
But I'm thankful her granddad was always near.

Defusing the Psychopath

Surveying your surroundings, calculating your
stance,
Bracing for the next shard, shattered in its
violent dance.
Speaking in muted tones, wary of tempers on the
edge,
Whispering silent prayers, clinging to life's
fragile ledge.

Trying to decide which wire to sever—
Is it the red one, or is it the blue?
Decoding the words that will neutralise,
The danger that's coming from you.

I nod—yes, I'm to blame for it all,
Yes, I deserve this storm's relentless call.
"I'll calm soon, and together we'll untangle this
thread",
But in my mind, I wonder which world birthed
your head?

Flashbacks shift between first-person and
bird's-eye view,
Leaving me to wonder—what did I ever do to
you?

Tell me, have you ever felt the wrath,
Of trying to defuse a psychopath?

The Illusion of Well-Being

"Oh you look great considering",
Even though what's hurting is now only
internally visible.
"Considering what you've endured, you look
brilliant",
If only you could see inside my mind, it's dark
and infinite!

My mind won't let my body eat,
My mind don't rest even when I sleep,
My mind it's on repeat,
Of scenes I don't wish to keep.

Considering you gave birth not long ago,
Considering the father to that child beat you half
to death not long ago,
Considering you found out that man lied and
cheated the whole time you know,
Considering you've got three broken ribs you
know …

You look good considering, I've heard it all.
I've been so close to the metaphorical edge and
losing it all.
Praying for intervention before I fall.

Asking for help, is it that easy to call?

Looking good and feeling good is entirely
contrary,
that feeling, I feel it, rarely.
Close my eyes and what follows is eerie,
"that's not superficial, I see it barely".

Why does my mind seep?
It flows and leaks,
Slowly until I weep,
Through my two porous holes, deep.

Once called my eyes,
Now windows to what's confined-
as beholders of the material you inscribed in my
mind.

But you know, you look good considering!

Echoes of my Former Self

I miss the chemistry,
But mostly, I miss my identity.

I miss the affection,
But mostly I miss my old reflection.

I miss the lust,
But mostly I miss the ability to trust.

I miss the warmth that used to be,
But mostly I miss the person I used to see.

Bliss to Abyss

Love felt like paradise,
Wrapped in his arms, a cherished prize.
The sound of his heart rising,
Quickening and tantalising.

Every glance was a promise,
Each kiss, a whispered vow.
In his embrace, time stood still,
A sanctuary where love could grow.

Nothing felt like this; now I must dismiss
The yearning for your kiss.
You're gone, lost to the abyss;
What once was bliss is now amiss.

My heartbeat now deafening, blaring,
Entering the courtroom, I'm glaring,
Seated there, no longer daring.
This situation is beyond comparing.

Hands shaking like leaves, I sit in disbelief.
My heart begins to settle; a relief—
Now I can finally hear the words of my brief,
Focusing on my breath, attempting to breathe.

Crosswords of Deception

Analytic in your answers, you're a crossword,
Yet all I receive from you are cutting cross
words.
And as a crossword tangles words and lines,
You endlessly construct puzzles in my mind.

Your words and actions become cryptic clues,
I decipher them obsessively, in columns and
hues.
Vertically, horizontally, I trace every act,
But nothing with you is ever simple or exact.

Nothing is black and white; I'm lost in the grey,
I can't fill in the blanks no matter what you say.
You're black, I'm white, yet still, I bruise—
Black and blue from the violence you choose.

"Family first!" you've inked on your skin,
But you know nothing of family within.
You treat love like a contract to bind,
My life, reshaped, forced to realign.

"R.I.P. Dad" carved into your chest,
But how would he feel, you yield that knife to
my breast?

You stood there, challenging fate,
My life in your hands, poised to abate.

I swear on my father's grave, I've stayed true,
But your words, once whole, are now fractured
in two.
You cover your lies, desperately reaching,
Never for me again—or the restraining order
you're breaching.

A Home Reclaimed

This home isn't broken just because there's no
man within,
In fact, it's the opposite—a fresh place to begin.
Yes, I've got a pot to piss in, and more than
that—
I'm living free from fear, in a space of peace and
bliss.

My children thrive without the constant strife,
I'd rather stand alone than let them live a chaotic
life.
No more listening to the rage, the cursing, the
fuss—
The best choice I made was to protect them from
us.

The Price of Protection

You missed her first smile,
You missed her first steps.
You've been gone for a while,
I harbour no regrets.

She has all she needs in this world,
Your choices created this distance,
I look in her eyes and I feel guilty that she will
never be daddy's little girl.
But her safety comes first in any instance.

www.ingramcontent.com/pod-product-compliance
Lightning Source LLC
La Vergne TN
LVHW021306200726
843509LV00012B/1804